Jim Arnosky

Hidden Wildlife

How Animals Hide in Plain Sight

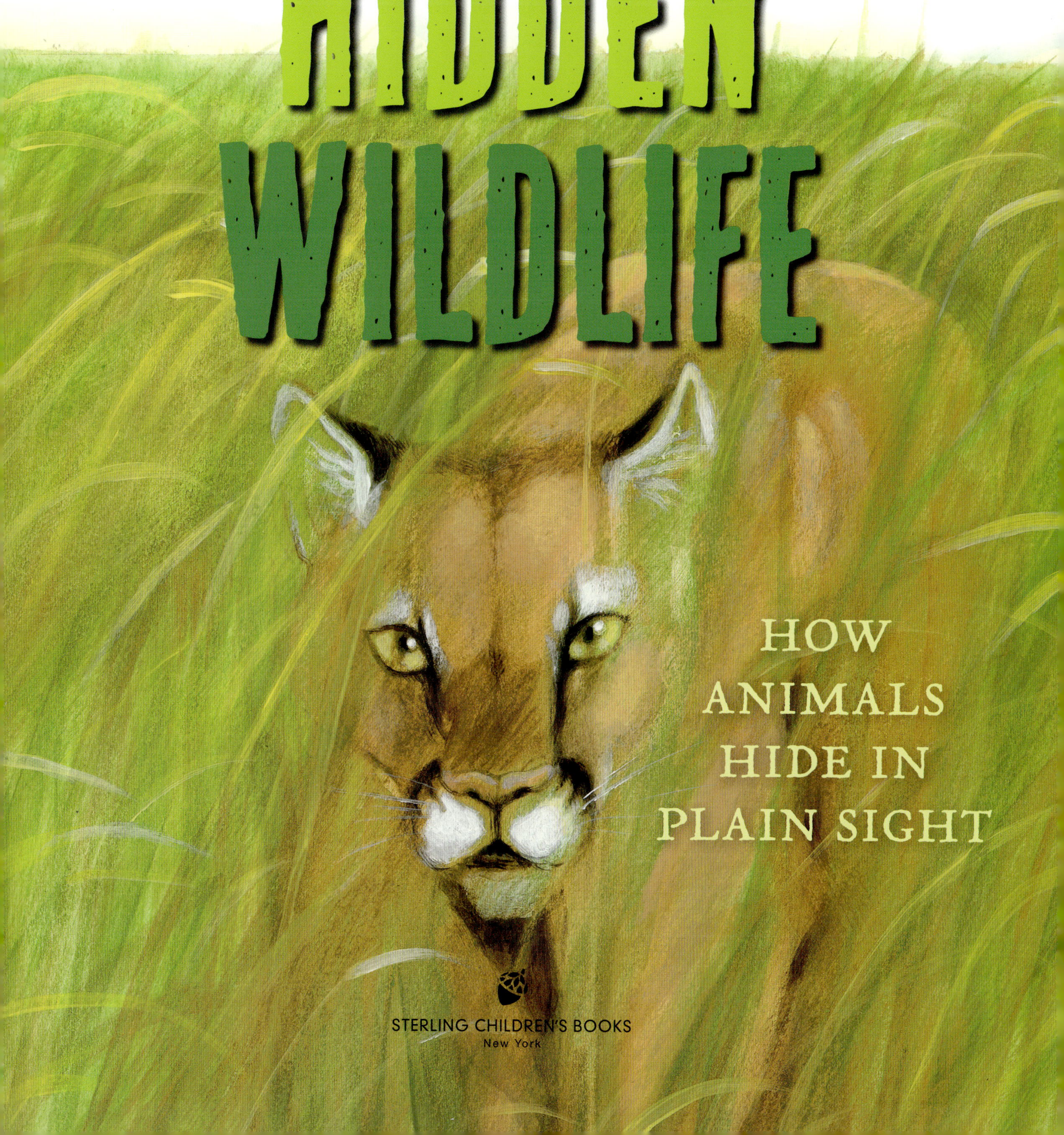

Sterling Children's Books
New York

For Pete Baker

STERLING CHILDREN'S BOOKS
New York

An Imprint of Sterling Publishing Co., Inc.
1166 Avenue of the Americas
New York, NY 10036

ISBN 978-1-4549-2097-7

Distributed in Canada by Sterling Publishing Co., Inc.
c/o Canadian Manda Group, 664 Annette Street
Toronto, Ontario, Canada M6S 2C8

For information about custom editions, special sales, and premium and corporate purchases, please contact Sterling Special Sales at 800-805-5489 or specialsales@sterlingpublishing.com.

Manufactured in China

Lot #:
2 4 6 8 10 9 7 5 3 1
06/17

www.sterlingpublishing.com

Design by Heather Kelly
The artwork in this book was created using pencil and acrylic paints.

CONTENTS

WHITE-TAILED FAWN

Introduction

In nature, predators and prey each instinctively know that to survive they must stay hidden from one another. For predators, this means being able to go unnoticed as they stalk their prey. For prey, this means being inconspicuous and difficult for hungry hunters to find.

The natural coloration of many animals matches their general surroundings, camouflaging them in their habitats. Some species are so well-camouflaged that they can hide in plain sight simply by staying still.

I find this most artful and beautiful aspect of animal survival so visually interesting that I want to paint every camouflaged animal I happen to spot in the scenery. My paintings of camouflaged animals in this book can be appreciated best when seen from a distance, the way you would see the animals outdoors. Prop the book open on a table so you can view each painting from across the room. Hold the book up so that others can also see the art this way. Practice visually separating the animals from the scenes I've painted them in, and you will become better at seeing camouflaged animals in the wild.

Jim Arnosky

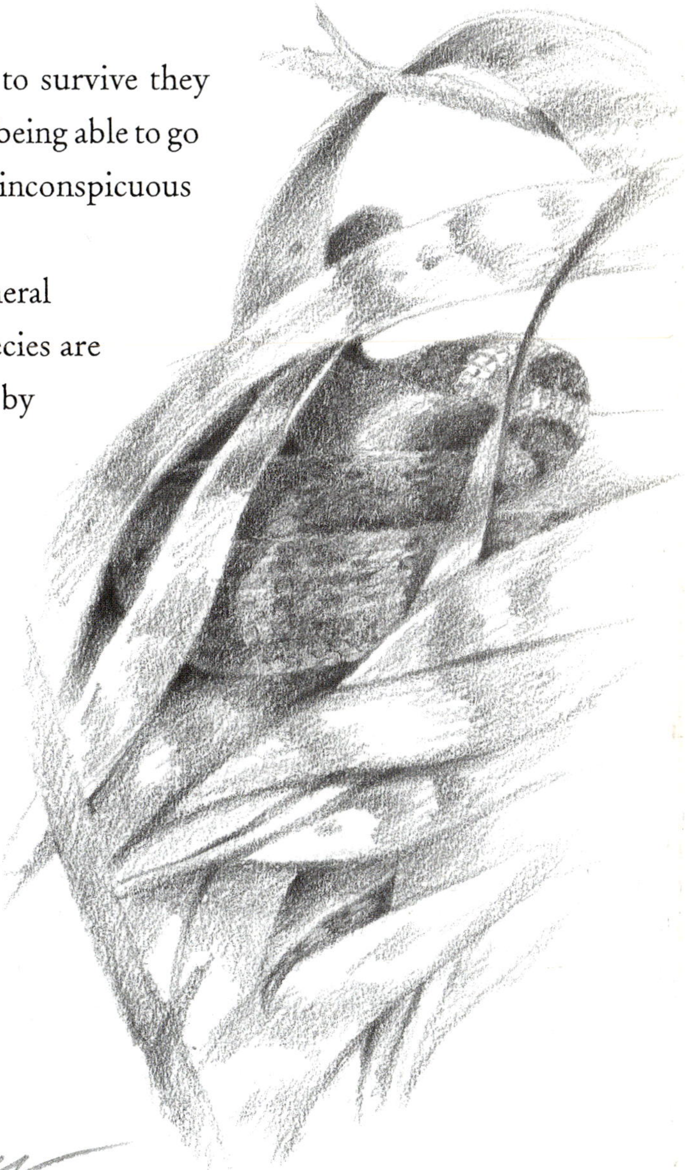

Animals can hide inside the scenery, blend in with it, or both, as this well-camouflaged water snake is doing.

As you can see in the painting at left, a fawn's white spots match the dapples of sunlight on the forest floor, where the young deer spends most of its time sleeping, curled up and perfectly still.

GREEN IGUANA

Rough green snake in green leafy tree.

SNAKE COLORS AND SHAPES

Snakes have the added advantage of coiling or slithering into different shapes. This further blends them into their surroundings. Here are five snakes that live in five different habitats. Prop the book open to view them while backing slowly away, and you will see them begin to "disappear" into their painted backgrounds. This is how difficult it can be to actually see them in the wild.

A copperhead's hourglass markings nearly duplicate the look of fallen leaves.

The northern water snake's squiggly markings combined with its smooth, flowing motion look very much like the water it swims in.

AMERICAN BITTERN

Reptile Camouflage

I was sitting on the edge of our dock in southern Florida when I spotted a large green iguana in the mangrove brush less than twenty feet away. The huge reptile—four feet long from nose to tail—was clinging to the top of a mangrove stump. The iguana's body shape, texture, color, and markings were perfectly camouflaged against the olive-brown bark and lime-green leaves. I would not have seen it at all had it not momentarily moved its head to face the sun. The lizard must have felt secure in its hiding spot because it paid little attention to me, even when I stood up to move my chair a bit closer.

Reptiles possess the ultimate camouflage. Their scaly bodies match the texture of the many different surfaces found in nature: trees, ground, and even water. And their distinctive species markings blend with the marks and crevices of wood, rock, and sand. How many elements in the scene at left are helping to hide the iguana?

Most lizards have some ability to alter their color. Hanging by its chin on the mangrove stump, the iguana near our dock gradually became darker and darker until it was as dark as the stump.

Chameleons are lizards that can change their color brilliantly and spectacularly by simply relaxing or exciting the cells of their skin to reflect sunlight at different angles.

The chameleon-like anole can change from dark brown to light green before your eyes.

The pygmy rattlesnake, also called a "ground rattler," is nearly invisible on pebbly ground. It is responsible for more snake bites to people than any other rattlesnake.

The broadly blotched pattern of the Burmese python blends with grass, brush, and water equally well.

Bird Camouflage

Camouflage protects birds when they are resting, nesting, or stalking prey. In birds, camouflage is created by individually marked feathers that, lying precisely together on the bird's body, combine to form spots, stripes, bars, or mottling. Think of it! Individual feathers, each with a pattern of its own, overlap with other feathers to create broader, bolder patterns. It is one of the most intricately beautiful inventions in nature.

The American bittern shown in the painting at left is well-camouflaged—note the long brown stripes that blend with the grasses along the water's edge. When this bird feels threatened, the bittern points its bill upward and stretches its long neck even longer to mimic the shape of the tall grass blades. This posture combined with the bird's camouflage stripes makes a bittern virtually invisible while standing out in the open.

While swimming, a duck's light-colored underparts make it less visible from below, where snapping turtles and large predatory fish dwell. Many perching birds also have light underparts, which include their breasts and throats. This dark-above/light-below combination presents a different silhouette shape every time the bird lands, making it difficult to locate visually as it flies from branch to branch through the brush.

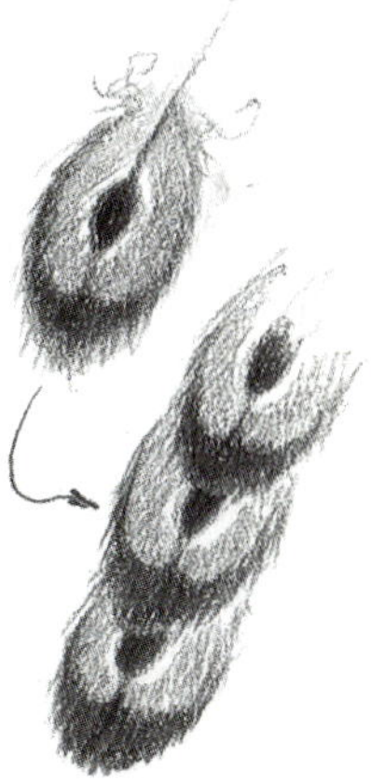

Above is an example of feathers combined for a mottled look.

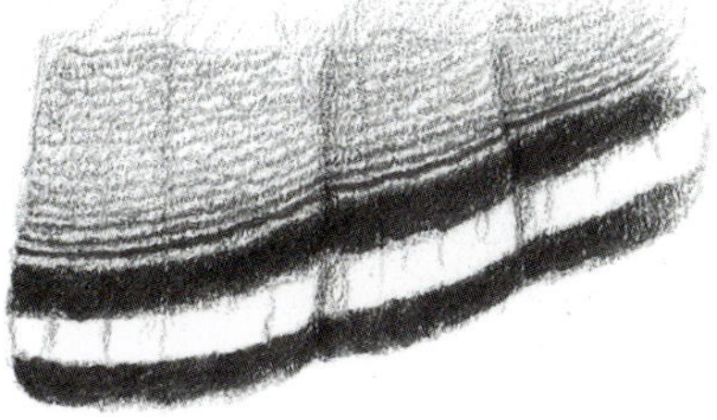

And here are feathers combined to form very fine stripes and bold bars.

A light-belly/dark-back combination presents a different silhouette depending on which way the bird faces.

The painting at left shows a bittern with its neck stretched tall.

The sketch here shows what a bittern looks like when it is not trying to hide.

The barred owl's vertical stripes look like the vertical stems and trunks of the small trees in their woodland habitat.

The ground-hugging woodcock has many different feather sizes, shapes, and patterns to blend perfectly with the fallen leaves. How many kinds of feathers do you see?

FEATHER PATTERNS AND COLORS

In many bird species, females are mottled in browns or grays to remain camouflaged and hidden in their nests, like the female red-winged blackbird at left. Their male counterparts are often brightly colored to draw attention away from the nesting females.

RED-WINGED BLACKBIRD

FEMALE WOOD DUCK

Ducklings' two-toned, light-and-dark coloration camouflages them while they are too young to fly.

ATLANTIC OCTOPUS

COLOR PLUS SUNLIGHT AND SHADE

In the sea, where there are few objects to hide behind, marine animals blend with water color, wave action, the seafloor, sunlight, and shade.

This shark's back is much darker than its white belly. But when the shark cruises near the surface, sunlight brightens its dark back, and its own shadow darkens the light belly. This creates little contrast between the back and the belly, and the shark appears transparent. This type of camouflage, called "countershading," allows the shark to hunt without creating a large, ominous silhouette in the water.

BLACKTIP SHARK

Against the colorful backdrop of a coral reef, even the brightest coloration can be camouflage. Tropical fish blend with rays of sun and also with the extra-dark shadows created by strong sunlight.

SCORPION FISH
The color and texture of a scorpion fish blends with the rocky bottom and coral mounds on the seafloor.

DAMSELFISH

SERGEANT MAJOR

SPOTTED TRUNKFISH

OWL BUTTERFLY

Camouflage in Marine Animals

Skates and rays are spotted or speckled to blend with the sun-dappled and sandy sea bottom.

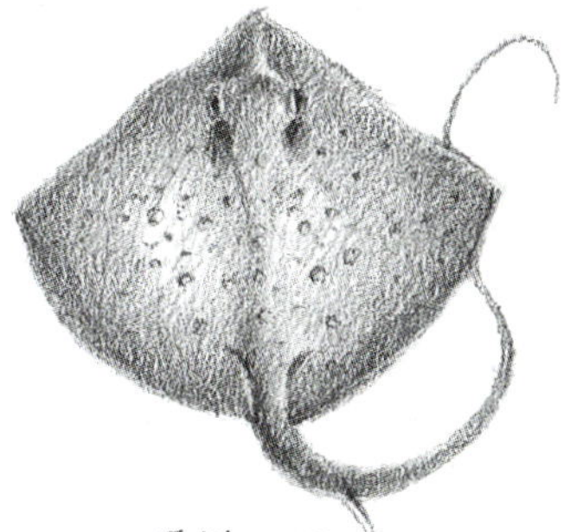

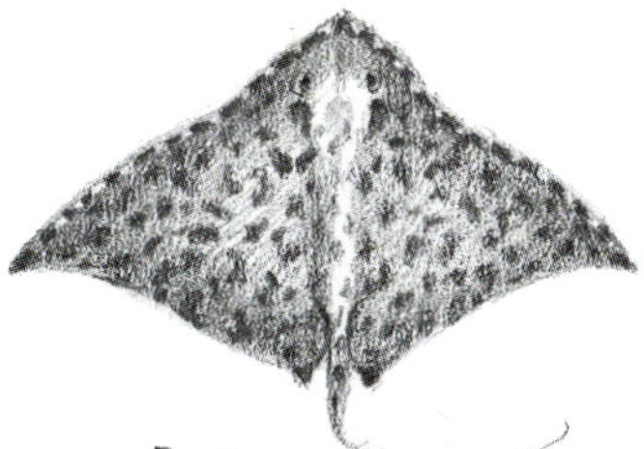

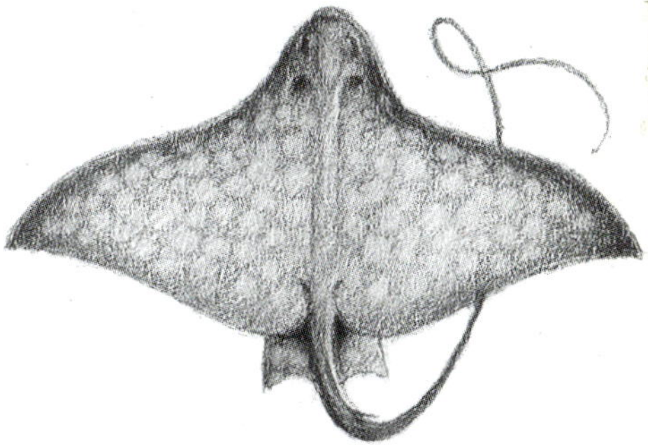

You rarely think of an octopus being near the beach in water only inches deep. But I watched the octopus you see at left in less than six inches of water as it crawled on the sandy seafloor only a few feet away from the dry beach. It was small, but it will eventually grow large enough to become one of the most formidable predators in the ocean. Aided by an uncanny ability to change its color to match any surface it moves over, an octopus will ambush small fish that swim near. In the short time I watched the little octopus, it changed from a light sandy color to a dark brown, and then, while it was resting near a chunk of broken reef, the octopus became purple to match the color of the coral.

Mollusks, such as the octopus and squid, change color by contracting muscles that pump pigment to their surface skin. It can happen gradually, as the animal moves slowly over the varicolored seafloor, or it can occur as rapidly as switching on a light, as in the case of squid swimming in the depths of the sea. Color changing can help marine animals stand out when communicating with others of their species or help them blend in as the animals camouflage themselves in their environs. Sea creatures that do not possess color-changing powers are camouflaged by their natural coloration and markings or by the reflective quality of their scales that mirror the water color.

In addition to changing its color, an octopus can also flatten its shape and close its eyes to meld with the seafloor.

Dolphins also have countershading as camouflage. And some species of dolphins have swirling stripes on their sides that resemble ocean waves.

All shiny, silver-sided fish mirror their surroundings. The reflection of sun, water, and sandy sea bottom on their scales masks the shapes of the fish.

On the seafloor, crabs blend with rocks and broken seashells simply by pulling their legs in close.

Insect Camouflage

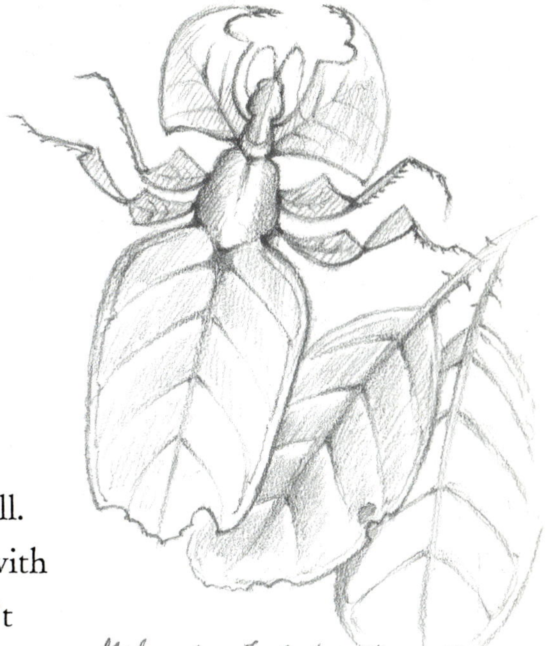

Malaysian Leaf Insect

I recently saw an owl butterfly for the very first time in a tropical butterfly aviary. It looked strange right-side up and also when it landed upside-down. Either way, it didn't look like a butterfly at all. It looked exactly like a great horned or long-eared owl, complete with ear tufts. The owl butterfly's camouflage pattern is one that doesn't blend into the background. It confronts you with two menacing eyeball-like markings designed to ward off any would-be predators.

Camouflage that mimics other creatures or objects is most common among insects. For example, walking stick insects look as if someone glued leaves and twigs together to form the shape of a large, long-legged bug.

Some insects have both blending camouflage *and* colorful stand-out markings. With its mottled brown wings folded closed, the underwing moth is almost impossible to see when it lands on tree bark. But when the moth wants to attract attention, it spreads its wings to reveal its brilliantly colorful and boldly marked underwings.

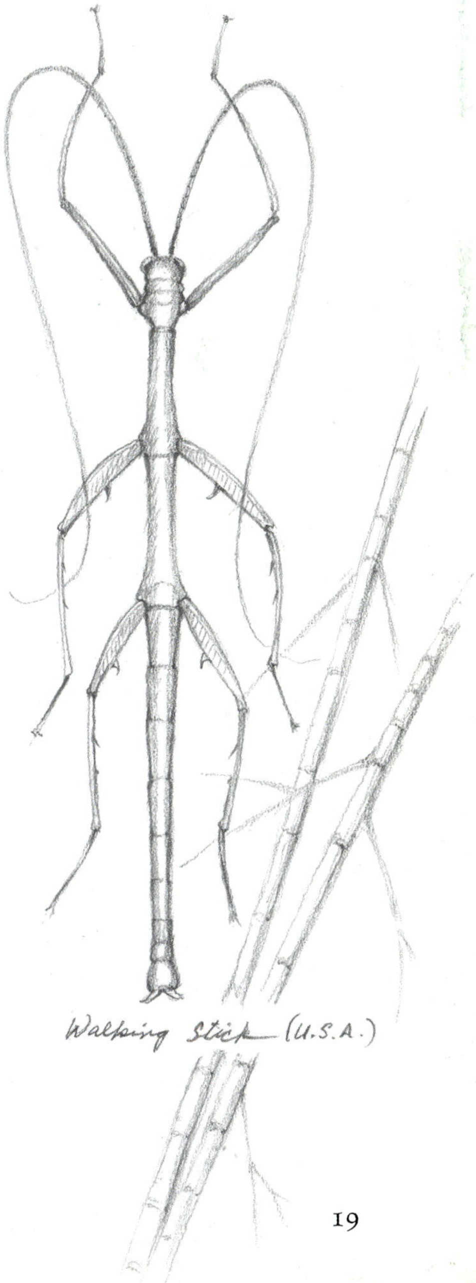

Walking Stick (U.S.A.)

Underwing Moth

Wings folded   Wings spread

Once you've seen a seven-foot-tall moose that, moments before, you thought was just another tree in the forest, the idea of Bigfoot also living there becomes more believable!

VANISHING IN THE FOREST

Solid brown and black animals are the hardest to see in the forest amid the shadows of trees. Even the largest animals can go unnoticed simply by standing still. And when you are lucky enough to spot one, it can seem to have vanished though it has only bent down or turned around, completely changing its shape.

markings, such as a raccoon's black mask and d tail, interrupt the raccoon's otherwise grayish tion, making the animal harder to notice in a woodland scene.

This chipmunk's black-and-white striped face and back blend with the bits and pieces of leaves and twigs on the woodland floor.

FLORIDA PANTHER

Dark
stripe
color
shady

Mammal Camouflage

In the Everglades, you can see an ocean of grass swaying rhythmically with waves of wind. I have often watched the grass there, looking for a glimpse of an ear, shoulder, back, or the long sweeping tail of a panther. I believe this will be how I see my first panther in the wild. And I have been training my eyes for that moment when suddenly, finally, I am able to spot the elusive cat slowly moving through the tall green blades.

It is surprisingly difficult to spot a tan-colored animal walking slowly through tall grass, even if most of the blades are a vivid green. In open sunny places, a panther's or deer's tawny coat blends and blurs into other sun-drenched elements of the scenery. In wooded areas, that same solid-colored coat can appear striped or spotted with the shadows of branches and leaves.

All mammals have fur or hair. Most wild mammals are solid tan, brown, gray, or black. Young wild mammals of many different species, including panthers, have spotted fur to better camouflage themselves while they are small and most vulnerable to predation. A spotted deer fawn can be so well-camouflaged that you can walk right by and never notice it.

A deer fawn's white spots blend with dappled sunlight.

The fawn's white spots fade over time, and by winter, it looks like its parents.

By ten weeks, the fawn has a solid coat like an adult deer.

As young animals grow, their natural coloration changes to better camouflage them in the broader world they will experience.

Mesmerized, the predator chasing the deer sees only the white flag. But when the deer abruptly lowers its tail, the flag suddenly disappears, leaving the predator confused. Meanwhile, the deer has gone running in a different direction, or is standing at a safe distance, completely camouflaged.

In northern climes, the best camouflage is that which changes with the season. Weasels change their coat in winter along with their name. A winter-white weasel is called an ermine.

SEASONAL COLOR CHANGES OF A SNOWSHOE HARE

Snowshoe Hare in Summer

Fall and Spring

Winter

The white-tailed deer is named for the white patch of hair on its rump and on the underside of its dark-brown tail. A deer bolting from danger raises its tail, flashing the white hair like a flag for other deer to follow, or to lure a pursuing predator into zeroing in on the white flag.

Long-tailed weasel in brown and winter white.

SNOWSHOE HARE
SUMMER AND WINTER

Seasonal Color Changes

Seasonal color changes in animals are caused by the reduction or increase of daylight hours each season, not by temperature change. Even in the warmest of years, the change of color from summer to winter and winter back to summer occurs on schedule, as the daylight hours grow shorter or longer. The color changes of the snowshoe hare, long-tailed weasel, Artic fox, and many species of birds happen gradually, over various parts of the animals' bodies. If you live where any of these animals live, you may have seen them in stages of changing from their summer to winter coats or plumage.

Mammals that change color seasonally change from mostly solid brown to all white. Birds change seasonal colors in more subtle ways to help them blend in with the more subdued colors of winter. The brilliantly yellow male goldfinch turns yellowish olive. The robin's red breast becomes rusty orange. With the advent of winter, the male wood duck's iridescent colors become muted. Small white feathers grow in to break up the strikingly bold markings of their summer plumage.

My favorite color change has always been that of snowshoe hares. Perhaps this is because we are Vermont neighbors. Every fall, I get to watch them change ever so slightly, day by day—brown to white and white to brown—each and every year.

A deer's winter coat blends with patches of remnant snow.

The willow ptarmigan of the far North makes four separate plumage changes a year to match the background colors of each Arctic season.

SNOW GEESE

Artful Nature

In spring, snow geese, which are white all year-round, nest on the brown grass of the Arctic tundra. The nesting geese would be conspicuous and vulnerable to predators were it not for the many white patches and goose-size lumps of remnant snow with which the white birds perfectly blend. And in the fall, when they fly southward at fifty miles an hour in large V-shaped formations through clouds, fog, and snow, their highly visible black wing tips help them spot each other and keep from crashing into one another.

Natural coloration helps animals stand out as well as blend in. And animal camouflage—beautifully designed to suit the habitat of each and every species—is natural coloration at its most artful best. Nature is the ultimate artist.

Author's Note

One afternoon I was videotaping a mother barred owl in a gumbo limbo tree. She was calling softly to her fledgling, which was perched unsteadily on a nearby limb. Suddenly, I heard the hum of a mosquito near my face, and I pulled away from my camera to brush the insect away. When I looked back through the camera's viewfinder, the owl seemed to have vanished. Then, slowly, my eye once again separated the owl's gray, striped plumage from the background of slim gray trees. And there it was, still in the exact same spot, centered in my lens.

Much of the effectiveness of camouflage depends on the eye of the beholder. Scientists who study the vision of animals have concluded that, while all fish, reptiles, and birds can see in color, not all mammals can. Some mammals see the world only in shades of gray. For them, pinpointing a camouflaged animal in the scenery must be very difficult, making them rely more on watching for signs of movement. All animals are easier to spot when they move. This is why even well-camouflaged animals freeze in the face of danger rather than flee.

When I began working on this book, I thought I'd be painting scene after scene filled with hidden animals. But the more I delved into the subject, the more I wanted to explore the idea of camouflage scientifically. I wondered *how* camouflage changed over the life of an animal and *what* exactly allowed certain animals to change their camouflage from scene to scene. In what ways do some northern animals turn white for winter? And why would an otherwise perfectly camouflaged deer have a huge white patch on its tail that made it stand out rather than blend in?

Questions like these led me on a fantastic voyage. This book became a kind of ship that I steered from one splendid island of beautifully camouflaged animals to the next. Researching, writing about, and painting these incredible creatures has made me look at the animal kingdom anew and appreciate more than ever how they survive and thrive in the world—very often hiding in plain sight.

More about Animal Camouflage

Arnosky, Jim. *Frozen Wild.* New York, NY: Sterling Children's Books, 2015.

Arnosky, Jim. *Shimmer & Splash.* New York, NY: Sterling Children's Books, 2013.

Franchino, Vicky. *Animal Camouflage.* True Books: Amazing Animals. New York, NY: Scholastic, 2015.

Jennings, Terry. *Camouflage.* Let's Find Out (Readers). London, UK: QEB Publishing, 2014.

Jenkins, Steve, and Robin Page. *I See a Kookaburra!* Boston, MA: Houghton Mifflin Harcourt Books for Young Readers, 2005.

Riehecky, Janet. *Camouflage and Mimicry: Animal Weapons and Defenses.* North Mankato, MN: Capstone Press, 2012.

Schwartz, David. *Where in the Wild?: Camouflaged Creatures Concealed... and Revealed.* Berkeley, CA: Tricycle Press, 2007.

Tildes, Phyllis Limbacher. *Animals in Camouflage.* Watertown, MA: Charlesbridge, 2000.

Underwood, Deborah. *Creature Camouflage series.* Portsmouth, NH: Heinemann, 2010.

Wood, Alix. *Amazing Animal Camouflage.* London, UK: Windmill Books: 2012.

Yaw, Valerie. *Color-Changing Animals (Animals with Super Powers).* New York, NY: Bearport Publishing, 2011.

Other Books in this Series

WILD TRACKS!
A Guide to Nature's Footprints

SLITHER AND CRAWL
Eye to Eye with Reptiles

THUNDER BIRDS
Nature's Flying Predators

CREEP AND FLUTTER
The Secret World of Insects and Spiders

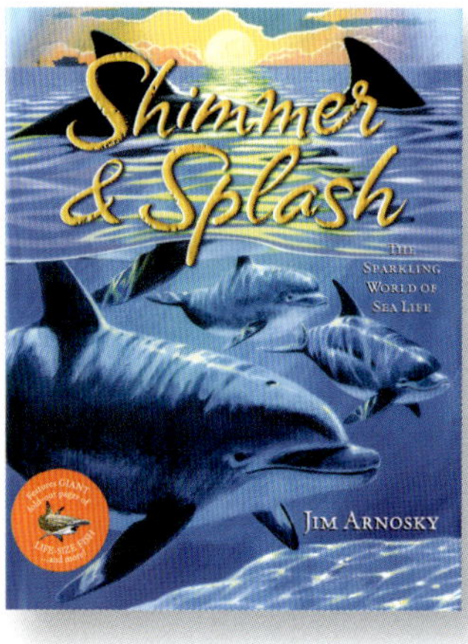

SHIMMER & SPLASH
The Sparkling World of Sea Life

TOOTH & CLAW
The Wild World of Big Predators

JIM ARNOSKY'S WILD WORLD

FROZEN WILD
How Animals Survive in the Coldest Places on Earth